SUMMARY

Dare to Lead

by

Brené Brown

Brave Work. Tough Conversations.

Whole Hearts.

Summary by: Kirsten Elsar

ISBN: 9781790547302.

Legal & Disclaimer

This book is only for informative and entertaining purposes. This is an exclusively composed summary, which refers to the original book. The information contained in this book and its contents cannot be amended, distributed, sold, used, quoted, or paraphrased without the consent of the author or the publisher.

Although the author and publisher have made every effort to ensure that the content and information contained in this book be compiled from sources deemed reliable, and it is accurate to the best of the author's knowledge, information, and beliefs, this book is not substitute for medical and professional advice. Please seek a professional if you have a health issue.

By reading the contents and information contained in this book, you agree that under no circumstances is the author and/or the publisher responsible for any losses, damage or disruption whether directly or indirectly, which are incurred as a result of the use of information contained within the book, including, but not limited to errors, omissions, or inaccuracies.

Contents

ntroduction 4

Summary and Analysis of the Book 5

Background of the Book.. 7

Part 1: Rumbling with Vulnerability.................................... 14

    Section 1: The Moment and the Myths 14

    Section 2: The Call to Courage.......................................20

    Section 3: The Armory..25

    Section 4: Shame and Empathy 40

    Section 5: Curiosity and Grounded Confidence...............48

Part 2: Living into Our Values 50

Part 3: Braving Trust 55

Part 4: Learning to Rise... 59

Conclusion.. 62

Action Plan... 63

Questions about the Book.. 66

Check out other summaries.. 67

Introduction

We are not brave anymore. Our leadership lacks courage. We try to lead with everything except our hearts. This is why there are so many examples of ineffective leadership around. We avoid being vulnerable because we equate it with weakness. *Dare to Lead: Brave Work. Tough Conversations. Whole Hearts* makes a case for allowing ourselves to be vulnerable to embark on a journey of true bravery. The book teaches us to take charge of both our personal and professional lives and stories by leading from the heart.

Summary and Analysis of the Book

The author still gets nervous before speaking in front of people. One of the tricks she utilizes is to keep the stage lights working only half of their full capacity. It assists her in observing the faces of the audience and witnessing their reactions to her words. She can connect with her audience this way. Her second trick has been derived from the stage-related advice of envisioning people to be naked while speaking in front of them. The author does not picture her audience naked but she pictures them in their personal spaces, at times with their vulnerabilities.

Before taking the stage to speak to people, the author reminds herself several times that she is going to be in front of just 'people.' When the author panicked before speaking to a high-profile audience once, another speaker reminded her that despite their position or field, the audience included people only. Seeing a couple of familiar faces in the audience and knowing their struggles and vulnerabilities at that moment, the author felt better and managed to connect with the audience on a deep level. The experience also helped her combine her interests i. e. meaning, bravery and connection with the corporate world. The author's career as a speaker also went through a major transformation after this event.

What Matters is the One who Tries, not the Ones who Criticize

The author refers to a quote by Theodore Roosevelt that praises the 'man in the arena'. The main idea of the quote focuses on the fact that it is the person who tries hard to do something that matters, not his critics. What matters is the hard-earned accomplishment that follows repeated attempts even after failure. Even if a person ultimately fails to do something after trying, he has failed after being greatly courageous. That counts for something.

Daring to be vulnerable does not take win or loss into account. It refers to the act of daring to try when we cannot know or dictate the result. The quote was the driving force behind the author's book *Daring Greatly*. Daring greatly always leads to some form of failure at a point. With great courage comes the possibility of a great fall. Our hearts might get broken on the path of great courage. It is extremely important to have the resilience to rise from such setbacks.

In this book, the author shares what she and her team have learned from some of the best leaders in the world.

Background of the Book

Goal of the Book

The goal of the author in this book is to share everything she has learned from two decades of research and experience and new research. The latter encompasses 150 interviews with C-level leaders on what leadership will mean in the future.

Definition of a Leader

The author considers a leader to be anyone who accepts accountability for discovering what individuals and processes are capable of. A leader is brave enough to help that potential develop.

The Need for Daring Leaders and Cultures of Courage

A sense of connectedness at the workplace is essential. According to top-level leaders that were interviewed for the book, what today's leaders need to succeed in a multilayered and complicated environment that keeps constantly transforming where it is critical to engage in innovation all the time includes two things.

These are more bravery in leaders and more courage in cultures. Th
leaders specified several reasons behind this. This includes motivatin
and encouraging innovation, thinking critically, combining an
evaluating information, growing trust, discovering shared politic
footing in an environment of extremely opposing views, being able t
make hard decisions, and a long list of other things.

According to the leaders, the ten cultural problems an
behaviors that obstruct the progress of organizations are as follows.

There is a lack of hard conversations and honest, fruitf
feedback. This lack and the culture of politeness lead to sever
complications and issues in organizations. It takes away clarity an
trust. The result is growing problems in the workplace since it create
two-faced behavior, back-biting and other such complications.

The second problem is that we end up giving all the time to th
management of erroneous behaviors instead of recognizing an
responding to the dread and emotions that stem from change an
chaos.

The third problem is the development of mistrust because c
no empathy or link between people.

Another issue is that a lot of people do not take calculated risks or map out and share fearless ideas to respond to transforming requirements and the ever-growing desire for innovation. Since people fear being made fun of for coming up with something new, it leads to the status quo.

Failures impede our progress and halt us because we end up excessively comforting those team players who are doubting their worth instead of dedicating resources to make amends and bring everything and everyone together.

It is a common practice to shame and accuse others rather than taking responsibility and learning sufficiently.

People choose to steer clear of discussions pertaining to inclusivity and diversity since they do not want to take any wrong step. This tendency to prefer comfort to tough discussions stems from privilege. It impedes meaningful transformation.

When issues arise, people tend to choose hasty and inefficient solutions rather than proper recognition and solution of problems.

Rectifying the wrong kind of mistakes creates a cycle of inefficienc and problem repetition, which has a huge cost.

Organizational values are blurred. We need real behavior instead of aspirations to evaluate them so that we can teach, quantif and assess these behaviors.

Since people are afraid and want to be perfect, they fail to lear and develop their skills.

The courage-forming skill sets needed by people to respond t these problems include the following:

Skills that Create Daring Leadership

1. The Vulnerability Rumble

Courage is not possible without vulnerability. We need to 'rumbl with vulnerability' to accomplish courage. Courage and fear can exis with each other. We can switch from fear to courage to achiev greatness. It is not bad to feel vulnerable. The word 'rumble' ha become extremely important in this context. It refers to a meeting o discussion that is dedicated to vulnerability. It is further dedicated t generosity and curiosity, to adhere to the chaos of identifying a problem and trying to solve it. It also pertains to choose a timeout and step back when required. It further means taking responsibility for our contributions without fear and to listen to others with as much enthusiasm as we wish to be heard with.

According to the author's research, courage consists of four skillsets. These include rumbling while staying vulnerable, living true to our values, encouraging trust and learning how to rise.

Rumbling with vulnerability provides the basis for the other three skills. We can only work on the other skills after working on our vulnerability skills. The author aims to help readers create the map for dwelling in these concepts by giving them the particular behaviors, procedures, activities, and tools required in this context.

The author and her team have tested this idea in fifty plus companies and with almost 10000 people who are getting familiar with these skills. This procedure has led to positive outcomes in companies including Shell, the Gates Foundation, Fortune 50 firms, different American military branches, etc.

2. Self-love and self-awareness help us be courageous

Courage is not an innate thing. Courage does not mean the absence of fear. Many leaders discuss experiencing fear all the time. Courage stems from how people respond to their fears. Experiencing fear does not impede progress. What impedes courageous leadership is the manner in which we react to our fear. How we think, behave and feel when we do not wish to rumble with vulnerability impedes our path to brave leadership. Exercising self-compassion and treating ourselves patiently are extremely significant to counter this.

3. Courage has a tendency to spread among people

To map out daring leadership and facilitate courage in firms and teams, we need to give rise to a culture in which courageous work, hard discussions, and complete hearts are part of the norm. This will help people feel secure and help the firm innovate and find solutions to problems. To be truly brave, leaders need to form connections with and deeply care about those working under them.

The Need for Caring and Connected Leaders

If a leader does not care about those working under him or her he or she needs to develop a connection of caring. If it does not work the leader should be substituted. It takes true courage to comprehend our own inability to be of service to those working under us. Today's leaders need to raise the current standards of leadership.

A very important category of leaders i. e. teachers need to comprehend that even though students require the armor of self-protection, there should some secure space in schools or classrooms where they can temporarily bid adieu to their armor for a short period of time and reveal their hearts. It can help them rumble with vulnerability to some extent. Shedding their armor this way might transform their lives. Hearts are at the heart of everything.

Everything Can Be Taught

No behaviors or patterns are hardwired. We can teach, note and measure anything at any age. Courage is not genetic. It can be earned.

Part 1: Rumbling with Vulnerability

Section 1: The Moment and the Myths

When the author read the Roosevelt quote for the first time, three lessons became clear.

1. Vulnerability in Light of Physics

If we are sufficiently daring, we will definitely fall at some point in time. Brave people do experience failure but they are willing to try despite that. We should be ready to take such risks despite the certainty of some failure since the reward is much more important than the failure.

2. Defining Vulnerability

When we are doubtful, in the middle of risk and exposed emotionally, we go through the emotion known as 'vulnerability.' The author clarifies based on her research involving thousands of people that even though people feel vulnerable during difficult times ulnerability does not equal weakness. The experiences that make us eel vulnerable are not easy at all. They can lead to anxiety and doubt. hey summon the phenomenon of self-protection. Dealing with these xperiences with a whole heart without any shield takes courage.

. Those that are not courageous themselves and just want to riticize do not matter

Those who want to criticize others for the sake of criticism vithout engaging in brave endeavors should not have a say in the natters of the brave and their opinions do not matter. They just want o ridicule others. We should only pay heed to the opinions that natter. The feedback of courageous people holds importance.

Don't pay heed to negative comments. Leave them. It's easy to e mean for people. Since it's not productive, let it be. We need to ind a balance since we can neither ignore all feedback nor consider all f it. If we shield ourselves from everyone's opinions, it translates into complete death. We should learn to take fruitful feedback into ccount.

How to Rumble: The Square Squad

Considering everyone's opinions will stop us from being brave
Ignoring all opinions will stop us from connecting with those who
matter. Compose a list of those whose opinions matter. Keep the lis
in your wallet and thank them simply for their honest opinions. Thes
should be the people who are honest enough with you in thei
opinions instead of trying to make you feel good about yourself whe
you are wrong. They should encourage you to be better. They shoul
love us because of our vulnerability and inadequacies. This is ou
square squad.

Six Myths Linked with Vulnerability

<u>**The First Myth: Vulnerability equals Weakness**</u>

Vulnerability is not synonymous with weakness because a
courageous acts involve the management of vulnerability.

<u>**The Second Myth: We don't Do Vulnerability**</u>

Emotional experiences, doubt and risk are common element
of our everyday lives. We cannot evade vulnerability. The onl
available choices involve handling vulnerability or it will handle us. I
we accept our vulnerability and choose to 'do' it knowingly, it mean

ve are learning to rumble with it and comprehending its role in directing our thoughts and behavior so we can align ourselves with our values and adhere to our integrity. If we choose to act like we are not vulnerable, it causes fear to take charge of our thoughts and behavior minus our input or knowledge, which leads to undesirable hields.

The Third Myth: Doing it Alone

People think they do not need vulnerability since they do not require anyone. We cannot survive alone since we are wired to form links. Our neurobiology makes us social. We need connections for authenticity.

The Fourth Myth: We can take Doubt and Emotion out of Vulnerability

People try to manage vulnerability by eliminating uncertainty and uneasiness from it by treating it as systematic. Sometimes they try to come up with apps to eliminate vulnerability. People need to comprehend that we cannot detach risk, doubt and emotional exposure from vulnerability. Even those whose jobs pertain to the elimination of vulnerability from systems need to learn to be courageous amidst vulnerability.

The Fifth Myth: Truth Precedes Vulnerability

People want to be secure before showing vulnerability. However, we need to have faith to enable ourselves to be vulnerable. We need to show vulnerability to build trust. We can trust those who have earned points gradually by supporting us over time. Trust builds slowly. Trust is a collection of moments on a step by step basis. It also involves mutual vulnerability over a period of time. For example, to build trust with our partners, we need to sacrifice our desires at times to support them. They need to do the same. Vulnerability and trust unfold in parallel.

The Sixth Myth: Vulnerability and Disclosure Go Hand in Hand

Vulnerability does not mean full disclosure. It needs sufficient and meaningful disclosure. In addition, vulnerability cannot be fake. It will eliminate trust from an equation. Our intentions should always be transparent. We should comprehend vulnerability constraints in relation to roles and interpersonal relations and define perimeters efining boundaries means underlining what's acceptable and what's ot and the reasons behind it. When leaders share, they need to do it ith a comprehension of their roles, identifying their professional nits, and clarifying their intentions and expectations because it will ot mean much without it.

eeling is Synonymous with Vulnerability

To feel things means being vulnerable. If we consider ulnerability to be a weakness, it means that we consider feeling to be weakness. This is wrong. The author's detailed research over a lot of ears taught her that vulnerability helps us live the experiences and notions that we seek. Vulnerability spawns love, a sense of elonging and pleasure.

Section 2: The Call to Courage

Clarity equals Kindness. Ambiguity equals Meanness

At times, we try to go a roundabout way before sayin
something since we do not want to hurt someone. This happens i
both our personal and professional lives. We believe that if we te
people the truth about something they are doing wrong; we will en
up hurting them. However, when we avoid straightforwardness to te
people half-truths to make them feel better about a situation, it
unkind. We always engage in such an act to save ourselves th
discomfort of telling the truth.

When a tough conversation happens, it is always helpful t
circle back after taking a break and thinking clearly about the issu
Such a break can help us analyze the issue and realize where we at
wrong.

When we fear something, or when an emotion invokes sel
protection, our thinking patterns are quite predictable. The firs
thought is that we are not sufficient. Then we proceed to think that
we honestly share the issue with our team, they will think less of us c
utilize the information against us. Then we think that we cannot b

onest about the issue since no one does that. We don't want to be he only ones in the limelight. Then we think that they are not honest bout what makes them afraid. They have a lot of issues too. Then we roceed to the thought that their issues and flaws caused us to face his. We think that the blame of the current situation goes to them nd they are trying to pin this on us. We end up concluding that we re better than them. Even if courage and faith are values important o us, fear can disrupt our synchronization with these values. We need o remember that what we fear can take us to our ultimate desire and estination.

Pursuing Treasure

When we are seeking the treasure of a decreased amount of ear and other related goals, permission slips can help immensely. In a meeting, permission slips mean every member giving himself or herself the permission to do or feel one thing for the meeting. These lips can make people open-minded to consider the points of view of ther people, regardless of how strongly they feel about what they believe in.

To avoid taking out our anger on other people and manage hings better, the following might help.

Four Core Lessons

A leadership team needs to have a combined comprehension o all the pieces in motion so that only one specific person is not th interlinking factor. Even when the leader is away, the team can kee meeting. A 'meeting minutes' process also helps improve matter Secondly, all team members need to join their efforts to approximat deadlines and timelines by rumbling till each member of the tear takes their ownership as a group. The author and her team use practice of time calculation and project preference that is known a 'Turn and Leave.' They utilize 'Post-it' notes to share their thought about the timeline of a project. In case they are handling differer projects, they list them in the order of priority. They show their slip at the same time to steer clear of the 'halo effect' and the 'bandwago effect.' The first pertains to everyone following the individual with th highest amount of influence. The second refers to the instinct to agre even when you wish to do otherwise.

We also need to avoid binary thinking that is common in firm People do not need to be divided into one-dimensional categorie They can be more productive without adhering to a stereotype. W

eed to consider determined facts and persistent faith. We need to
dream but check those dreams with facts.

Readiness to apologize for mistakes is an extremely important
skill in the context of leadership as well. A leader should follow this
with rectifications. Scrutinizing one's part also holds importance in the
context of the rumble procedure.

Serving Others: Powerful and Wise

Loneliness, compassion and empathy are not usual components
of leadership training but they are quite real. If leaders do not spend a
considerable amount of time addressing fears and feelings, they will
end up spending a huge amount of time handling inefficiency and lack
of productivity. We need to be courageous enough to have curiosity
and cover the kind of feelings and emotional episodes that people
find themselves unable to express or what might go beyond their
awareness.

When a person is having a problem repeatedly, we need to get
to the bottom of the problem. We need to pay heed to what they are
saying. Don't rush to share your opinion or thoughts. Don't indicate
to the speaker that they need to stop talking. Let them talk peacefully.

We also need to define some boundaries. People are allowed to b

angry or sad but their emotions should not direct their behaviors in a

unacceptable direction. We should not allow anyone to yell, interrup

others, roll their eyes, put others down, etc.

If a rumble becomes too much, take a time-out. People ca

relax for 10 minutes or so. Even if someone else asks for a break, w

should allow it because it will improve the quality of our decisions

We cannot regulate others' feelings.

Daring leadership aims to serve others. It is not selfish

Courage takes precedence.

Section 3: The Armory

According to Minouche Shafik, jobs pertained to muscle
earlier. They come from the brain now. In the future, they will relate
to the heart. The heart lies at the center of all shields and protective
layers. The heart is the most prized piece of the human experience.
The heart personifies our ability to love and be loved back.

The Benefit of Wholeheartedness

Brené Brown calls existing with a heart that has no armor
'wholeheartedness'. It refers to the existence of worthiness. It means
gathering the courage, compassion and link to start every morning
with the thought that regardless of how much we do or don't, we are
sufficient. It also refers to the process of ending our night with the
thought of accepting our imperfections, fear and vulnerabilities and
realizing that we are courageous and deserve love and connectedness
despite that.

Integration

Wholeheartedness means getting rid of the protective shields
around our hearts and involving integration. It involves integration

between our thoughts, feelings and behaviors. It pays attention to our entire messy selves. A lot of organizations focus on encouraging people to bring their entire selves to work but they do not actually practice it. They will want people to separate their hearts and bid goodbye to their vulnerability. They want people to leave the mess behind and be less human. Such cultures require the development of armor and reward it.

In cultures where vulnerability and emotions are considered to be liabilities, the heart is supposed to be closed off. By keeping the heart caged, we murder courage. We need our emotional heart to keep pumping vulnerability and encourage trust, accountability, creativity and innovation. The disconnection from our hearts leads to a loss of control. On the contrary, an open heart and a strong connection with our emotions give rise to new avenues and arenas. It also improves critical thinking and decision-making and what follows includes resilience, self-compassion and empathy.

Our ego fights with our heart. It does not want us to feel vulnerable or uneasy. Since we wish to shield our ego, we try to create armor when we don't have sufficient responses or feel like we are wrong. We don't want others to misconstrue or judge us. We don't want people to think we are weak.

We don't want to feel Shame

What challenges our ego and self-worth the most is 'shame'. Shame makes us feel so faulty that we end up doubting our own worth of being loved. The antidote to shame is empathy. We are giving rise to cultures that cage the heart and stop us from capitalizing on presents including empathy, emotional mastery and vulnerability. Machines do some things better than us because they have no ego and can calculate and compute rapidly. However, we will always be better at many tasks if we allow ourselves to be daring in our leadership and capitalize on our biggest asset i. e. our heart.

Sixteen Types of Armored Leadership and the Daring Leadership Response

Armored Leadership

Armored leadership seeks perfectionism and dreads failure. Perfectionism does not focus on self-improvement or excellence. It seeks approval. Perfectionism wants to avoid shame by doing things perfectly and seeming perfect.

Daring Leadership

Daring Leaders practice and promote healthy determinatio and struggle, self-compassion and empathy. Having conversatior about perfectionism and discussing problematic signs and behavior can help.

Armored Leadership

Most of us have a tendency to taint moments of joy b dreading possible tragedies or mishaps. The moment we achiev something, we have a moment of joy, which makes us incredibl vulnerable. We counter that feeling of vulnerability by being afraid c what could go wrong.

Daring Leadership

We can handle the above act of Armored Leadership b practicing gratitude and celebrating wins and milestones the way the should be celebrated. We should express our gratitude by tellin others or writing it down somewhere. We can even share gratitud with our family members over dinner. Personifying and practicin ratitude can transform our lives. Gratitude is realizing and elebrating something worth losing. We can begin or finish meetings y sharing an example of gratitude each, which can build trust and orm links.

Armored Leadership

All of us have a way of numbing ourselves. We use different vays to do it including food, television, social media, etc. When we tilize these channels of numbness, they translate into addiction. We ry to take the edge off and numb our emotions. If we take the edge off emotions such as pain and uneasiness, we will also end up numbing emotions such as joy, love and others that add meaning to our lives.

Daring Leadership

Daring leadership is about defining boundaries and discovering comfort in the true sense of the word. Vulnerability, anxiety, and resentment make us pursue numbing. Resentment is always linked with absent boundaries. To avoid numbing, we need to tap into discomfort.

When we are feeling edgy, we need to ask ourselves about such feelings and their cause. Then we should proceed to the real source of comfort and reset for us instead of numbing. For example, we can prevent comfort eating by walking if that would bring us real comfort. We can use worker assistance programs in the context of boundaries, proper rumbles with vulnerability and how to soothe anxiety.

Armored Leadership

Many of us practice the 'Victim or Viking' philosophy and adhere to this binary form of thinking. This requires doing everything one can to curb emotion and exercise control over others. This form of thinking makes people act like if they want to survive, they have to be in a fighting and clashing mode all the time.

Daring Leadership

Daring leadership works differently and involves integration. I creates a strong back but keeps the front soft. It also allows the heart to be wild. To avoid the above fake binary ways, the answer is to utilize integration. It involves combining all our components. We can be soft and hard in parallel, afraid and courageous at the same time etc. The recommended practice by the author is strength in the back oftness in the front and wildness in the heart. According to the author, a strong back stems from grounded confidence and clear boundaries. A soft front refers to the act of curiosity and vulnerability. A wild heart originates from existing despite the issues and complexities of existence and not falling victim to anything that decreases our value as a human.

Armored Leadership

We want to know everything and be right all the time. It can be a huge burden and give rise to a lack of trust, decrease the quality of decisions, and lead to unneeded rumbles and conflict that don't spawn fruitfulness. People utilize being a knower to shield themselves against shame and tough situations.

Daring Leadership

Daring leadership focuses instead on being a learner properly. Three strategies work in this context. Underline the issue clearly. Prioritize learning curiosity skills. Recognize and reward people for good questions and examples of when they acknowledge that they do not know something but wish to discover it. This is a personification of daring leadership behaviors.

Armored Leadership

Armored leadership uses cynicism and sarcasm to hide behind it.

Daring Leadership

Daring leadership entails three steps to act against sarcasm and cynicism.

Firstly, practice clarity and kindness. Have the courage to voice what you mean and mean what you utter. If cynicism and sarcasm conceal hopelessness, then the opposite is to nurture and foster hope.

Armored Leadership

Armored leadership utilizes criticism in two usual forms to protect itself. The first way is to utilize nostalgia or using the past to shield against new ideas. The second is to use the word 'we' as an invisible army. For example, saying that 'we' don't like the new idea. Fear often breeds criticism.

Daring Leadership

A daring leader contributes and takes risk instead of criticizing. He or she plays an active part in the happenings.

Armored Leadership

Power is not bad itself. However, when 'power over' dynamics exist and people use power over others, it leads to issues.

Daring Leadership

Daring leadership utilizes power with, to and within. 'Power with' refers to the act of discovering common points among dissimilar interests to develop shared strength with the assistance and acknowledgement of and respect for dissimilarities, collaboration, cohesion and shared support. 'Power to' means giving roles to each person on the team and recognizing their distinctive potential. 'Power within' is the capacity to notice differences and respect other people. It has its concrete roots in self-knowledge and self-worth.

Armored Leadership

When people do not know their strengths and their area o delivery, they hustle and try to be everywhere to have a sense o belonging even when they cannot deliver in a specific area.

Daring Leadership

Daring leadership is about comprehending our worth. It entai meeting all team members and rumbling with them about the distinctive contributions. These reminders of where everyone i strong are effective because sometimes people forget their strengths.

Armored Leadership

Armored leadership focuses on compliance and contro stemming from power and fear.

Daring Leadership

Daring Leaders inspire commitment and mutual purpose. Eve in the kind of industries that are compliance-driven and tightl regulated, daring leaders formulate context and communicate it t others. They explain the reason behind specific strategies and hov tasks are connected to current preferences and mission.

The **Accountability and Success Checklist or the TASC approach** can help in this context.

T asks the question about the owner of the task.

A proves as to whether they have the authority to be held accountable for the task.

S asks whether there is an agreement regarding the setup including resources, time and clarity being sufficient for success.

C inquires as to whether a checklist exists regarding the required events to achieve the task.

Armored Leadership

Armored leadership approaches uncertain times by making the most of fear and doubt and using it against people.

Daring Leadership

Daring leadership recognizes, names and normalizes shared fear and uncertainty but it neither strengthens discord nor takes advantage of it.

Armored Leadership

Armored leadership celebrates and rewards fatigue and sleeplessness since it considers work to be more important than sleep. It considers exhaustion to be a status symbol. It further equates fruitfulness with self-worth. This leadership considers time spent with one's family to be a waste.

Daring Leadership

Daring leaders consider rest, play and recovery to be extremely significant. They prefer a diverse timetable instead of just exhausting oneself to death. Rest and play leave a substantial effect on our productivity. Play sustains our mental health and affects our brain in a positive way.

Armored Leadership

Armored leaders allow discrimination, a culture that supports itting-in' and pursuing approval. People have to change who they are > fit in.

Daring Leadership

Daring leaders promote a sense of true belonging, diversity and iclusivity. People can be themselves since such leadership respects iverse viewpoints.

Armored Leadership

Armored leaders are concerned with the collection of gold ars. Medals and stars are acceptable in a person's early career path ut once a person enters management and leadership, these should ot be their goal.

Daring Leadership

Daring leaders give others gold stars. They reward others istead of focusing and seeking to be rewarded themselves. eadership needs to be their priority.

Armored Leadership

Armored leaders engage in zigzagging and avoiding instead of just doing the hard thing. They avoid vulnerability this way.

Daring Leadership

Daring leaders save time by doing what needs to be done. They are straightforward and take actions no matter how difficult situation seems.

Armored Leadership

This includes leading from hurt. Such leaders do not feel rewarding connection with their family and try to compensate for it by being all the more weighty at work. They try to steal credit for things they have not done. They try to compensate for the pain of not being praised by their parents or even make up for the professional disappointment of their parents' lives if any.

Daring Leadership

Daring leadership leads from the heart. It does not focus on superficial elements. It focuses on what needs to be done.

Section 4: Shame and Empathy

Vulnerability is so difficult because the hardest thing is shedding our armor and exposing our heart. It can bring us face to face with shame. Our ego fails to comprehend that impeding our emotional growth and closing down our vulnerability will make shame, detachment and isolation our destiny instead of protecting us from it.

Shame is known as the 'master emotion.' It makes us feel that we are never sufficient. Its power is matchless since it can make us feel unworthy of love, belonging and connection.

The Basics of Shame

All of us have shame. It is primitive and a widespread phenomenon. The only people who do not feel shame are devoid of the ability of human connection and empathy. In other words, only sociopaths don't have shame.

None of us wants to discuss shame. It makes everyone uneasy. The power shame has over us is directly proportional to how much we try to avoid discussing it.

Shame is related to the fear of disconnection. It stems from the feeling that some wrong step we have taken or a right step we failed to take has rendered us undeserving of connection. Shame refers to the extremely agonizing feeling of thinking that we have faults that make us undeserving of connection, love and belonging.

Some of the things that make people feel shame include being angry at their children, getting fired when they are expecting their firstborn, getting demoted sometime after being promoted, concealing their addiction, failing their business after their friends invested in it, etc. It also involves being called a loser in front of one's colleagues, being asked for a divorce, being sexually harassed but not being able to say anything, and so on. According to neuroscience research, shame can cause physical pain.

The Difference between Shame, Guilt, Embarrassment and Humiliation

We use these four terms interchangeably even though they are different. This makes it all the more difficult to talk about shame. The difference between shame and guilt is that guilt relates to doing something bad while shame relates to considering yourself to be bad.

People do the mistake of using shame as a moral compass fo behavior. This practice can give rise to immoral, wounding an damaging behavior. Shame has a correlation with aggression, violence addiction, depression, bullying, and eating disorders. Guilt has negative correlation with these outcomes. Guilt contains values an empathy. This is the reason why it enjoys immense power and th quality of social adaption.

We also confuse humiliation for shame. Humiliation come before shame and can turn into shame but is not as damaging Embarrassment is passing in its nature since we are aware that other have also done the same thing. It is not as severe as the othe emotions mentioned above.

The Faces of Shame at Work

Some of the by-products of shame at work includ perfectionism, back-channeling, gossiping, favoritism, harassmen bullying, comparison, cover-ups, blaming, discrimination, self-wortl linked with productivity, 'power over' dynamics and teasing. Ever when people need to leave, they should be allowed to do it in dignified way. Shame works in a methodical manner.

Shame Resilience

We need to develop shame resilience. It refers to the capacity to exercise legitimacy when we go through shame, to navigate the experience without affecting our values, and to rise from the 'shame' experience with amplified connection, compassion and bravery. Shame resilience refers to the ability to shift from shame to empathy, the latter being the actual remedy to shame.

Empathy and its Value

Empathy should not be confused with sympathy. It is the foundation of the cultures of trust and connection. Empathy does not entail the link to an experience. It involves linking to the emotions underlining an experience.

The five skills of empathy are as follows:

1. To view the world as others view it or take perspectives. Diverse perspectives help us see and comprehend what the world and its people are about.

1. To start being non-judgmental.

2. To comprehend the feelings of other people.

3. To express our comprehension of another person's feelings

4. To practice mindfulness. It refers to the adoption of a balance manner toward negative emotions to avoid crushing c overstating feelings.

Don't do the following if you want to practice empathy:

- Avoid sympathy. Practice empathy instead. Empathy mear feeling people's pain. Sympathy entails feeling sorry for ther and breeds disconnection.

- Don't gasp and be in awe of what someone else ha experienced.

- Don't treat someone like they have had a major fall. Don't te them you never expected them to fall like this.

- Don't try to blame and tackle someone else for your friend fall.

- Don't treat your friend like they cannot make a mistake. Don't tell them that they are wonderful and it's not as bad as it looks.

- While saying to someone suffering that 'Me too, you are not alone' is great and forms a connection, shifting focus to you is not good. Don't make it about yourself.

How to Practice Empathy

Practice empathy. Make mistakes. Return to the start. Rectify the mistake. Be better.

Self-compassion

To practice empathy, we first need to build self-compassion. We need to be generous to ourselves instead of trying to shame or punish ourselves for our errors.

Converse with yourself like you would with a loved one. You will stop saying things to yourself you would never tell anyone else.

Empathy

Tell people you feel them, they are not alone, you see them you have been in a place like this and it's really difficult, me too, yo understand what it's like, etc.

Empathy and Building Shame Resilience

The four skills of shame resilience are as follows:

1. Identify shame and comprehend its triggers.

Some of our shame shields include moving away from peopl or withdrawal, moving toward people to please them and movin against people in aggression. We need to get rid of these.

2. Adopt critical awareness

This involves seeing that you are not the only one and you ar normal.

3. Connect with others

When we reach out to others, we know that what makes us feel shamed is quite common

. Communicate shame

Staying quiet feeds shame. Express it and you will curb it.

Section 5: Curiosity and Grounded Confidence

Grounded confidence entails learning and letting go o
learning, trying and failing and enduring some losses. This type o
confidence does not include conceit or superficial elements. It stem
from the foundation of self-awareness and experience. When w
comprehend how courage can change our leadership, we can let go o
the armor that burdens us to pave the way for grounded confidenc
that encourages and assists us in our journey of being brave.

The paradoxes that incite vulnerability in leaders include a bi
heart and hard decisions, positive thinking and suspicion, modest
and solid tenacity, left brain and right brain, letting chaos rule in th
process of formation and controlling chaos in the process of scaling
speed and quality when creating something new, simplicity and
selection, speed in business-formation, aiming high but taking a smal
start, thinking internationally but acting locally, both short- and long
term, driven goals and attention to detail. Leaders need to form skill
to handle these paradoxes properly. Easy learning does not give rise to
solid skills. It is not easy to develop rumbling skills but it's worth it.

Desirable hardship is when the brain needs to go through some
uneasiness while learning. Grounded confidence is the sum of rumble

ills, curiosity and practice. Curiosity results from vulnerability and courage. Curiosity has a correlation with intelligence, creativity, better learning and memory, and problem-solving. Curiosity transforms our brain's chemistry. It improves our ability to learn and preserve information. However, curiosity makes us uneasy since it entails vulnerability and doubt.

Curiosity involves spending as much time with a problem as possible instead of focusing on the solution only. In sum, rumbling skills, the grounded confidence to get rid of the armor, curiosity and learning can drive greatness.

Practice vulnerability, become self-aware, and have difficult discussions. The 'Dare to Lead' section on Brenébrown.com can guide readers about more rumble tools.

Part 2: Living into Our Values

The Significance of Values

Life or the arena can be extremely confusing in difficult time We feel the need to prove our worth to those around us. Distractior can confuse us. Our toughest critics can demoralize us. We might fe the need to stop trying. In such times, we need to keep our values i mind since we might fail to name those in difficult times.

A value refers to a manner of existing or thinking that w consider being really significant. Dwelling into our values mear practicing them instead of just saying them. It means we synchroniz our purposes, sayings, thinking and actions with them.

First Lesson

Name your values. You can only have one collection of value for your personal and professional aspects of life.

Second Lesson

Convert your values from words to behavior. Don't just talk about them.

Third Lesson

Empathy and self-compassion are the most important

To succeed as a brave leader, we only need a couple of people who comprehend our values as an act of empathy and support us. We need self-compassion to celebrate ourselves because without it, no one else will.

Dwelling into Our Values and Feedback

Giving Feedback

A very difficult situation is to stay synchronized with our values while offering and receiving feedback. The following can help.

1. We are ready to give feedback when we sit with/next to someone instead of across from them.

2. We are ready to give feedback when we put the issue in front of us and the receiver instead of between us.

3. We are ready to give feedback when we are ready to listen, ask queries, and embrace that we might not comprehend the issue completely.

4. We are ready to give feedback when we are ready to admit what the other person excels at instead of just underlining their mistakes.

5. We are ready for feedback when we are ready to identify the other person's strengths and how they can utilize them to respond to their hurdles.

6. We are ready for feedback when we can hold the other person responsible minus blaming or shaming them.

7. We are ready for feedback when we are ready to admit our part in the issue.

8. We are ready to give feedback when we can sincerely thank the other person for their hard work instead of just condemning them for their shortcomings.

9. When we are ready to discuss that finding a solution to these hurdles can give rise to growth and products.

10. When we are ready to have and show the vulnerability and openness that we want to see from the other person.

Receiving Feedback

The key to receiving feedback properly and skillfully is to listen, integrate it and echo it back with accountability.

Knowing Values Equals Knowing People

People don't exist without their values. We need to know and comprehend their values to know them.

Operationalization

Be courageous.

Do the work.

Take great care.

Part 3: Braving Trust

Trust and Lack of It.

Trust or lack of it can change people substantially. If we question people in a way that they don't feel that we trust them, we can turn them into a machine in a matter of seconds. It can activate their shield and armor, shut down their heart and turn their defenses on. This lockdown can take away our ability to see or comprehend anything since we are on a path of emotional survival.

We need to have a talk in which we assure the other person that we trust them completely and avoid the trust talk that activates their trust shield. We need to be particular about any problematic behavior instead of pointing fingers at someone's character and talking about trust and trustworthiness generally. This will facilitate true change.

Rumble Tool Known as the Braving Inventory

The author utilizes the braving inventory so that each perso fills it separately and then meets one another to discuss the similaritie and dissimilarities between their experiences.

Setting Up Boundaries

It is about respecting each other's boundaries. We need to as questions in case of any ambiguities. We shouldn't hesitate to say no.

Staying Reliable

When you say you will do something, you will do it. You w stay knowledgeable about your abilities and shortcomings so that yc won't promise things that you will not be able to deliver.

Staying Accountable

It encompasses accepting your mistakes, apologizing an rectifying them.

Acting as a Vault

You don't share information and secrets about other people that's not your place to share. You don't violate the rules of confidential requirements.

Having Integrity

You choose courage over easiness. You do what's right instead of what seems enticing.

Practicing Non-judgment

It entails both parties asking for assistance without judging each other.

Being Generous

You interpret what people intend to do, say and act like with the highest degree of generosity possible.

The Use of the Inventory to build Self-Trust

We can use this inventory in the context of developing self trust as well. In this case, we will apply all the above seven elements t ourselves.

Part 4: Learning to Rise

Teach People How to Land

We need to teach people how to handle difficult landings when we are encouraging them to jump from the sky. It is extremely unfair to people if we ask them to be courageous and come face to face with the possibility of failure without teaching them how to land.

When we are brave enough to enter our story and own it, we will get a chance to compose the ending. When we refuse or fail to own our tales of hindrances, pain and failure, they will end up owning us.

The Reckoning

The first important term in this context is 'the reckoning.' The reckoning entails the way we walk into a difficult story. It refers to the knowledge that we are emotionally hooked and being curious about his feeling. We unload pain in different ways which include 'chandeliering' or having an outburst with the slightest trigger, using our pain to blame others and lash out, numbing pain and storing it.

Other strategies include pretending or acting like nothing is wrong and trying to deny our feelings since we are scared of getting stuck.

Reckoning Strategies

Inhale through your nose deeply, filling your stomach, and count till four.

Hold that breath in and count till four.

Exhale the air completely through your mouth but keep it slow. Contract your stomach. Count till four.

Hold your empty breath and count till four.

The Power of Calm

Practice the superpower of calm since it gives birth to perspective and mindfulness while handling emotional reactivity.

The Rumble

The rumble is where we take the story we entered and own it. we don't have data, we will always end up fabricating stories. The st tale we weave is known as the "shitty first draft" or SFD. Fear mpletes the gaps in our SFDs. This is worrisome because stories at do not have a lot of real data end up having lots of fictional data. e end up mixing it into a lucid, emotionally satiating type of reality. nese stories are known as conspiracy theories. The next step is nfabulations, which are lies told honestly. We believe it's based on cts but it's based on our opinion only. It might have an iota of data it but a majority of it is our fear. We need to stop our SFDs from rning into conspiracy theories and then confabulations. The most rmful stories include the ones that threaten our 'creativity', 'divinity' d 'lovability'. We need to engage in a story rumble by utilizing the eviously discussed tools for developing courage.

We need to rise. We need to give rise to a revolution in this orld of cynics by getting rid of our armor, rumbling with lnerability, dwelling into our values, being courageous and trusting ith open hearts, and rising to take charge of our own tales. We need rebel and for that we need courage.

Conclusion

In sum, Brené Brown teaches us to let go of our shields and l brave. We need to be vulnerable and brave and give rise to tl cultures of courage so that others can also follow the same path. Th will help us let go of armored leadership, open our hearts ar embrace daring leadership. When we own our stories, we will be ab to dictate their end. Ultimately, being brave, staying vulnerabl adhering to our values and encouraging trust will help us rise. If v follow the advice offered in the book, we are destined for greatness.

Action Plan

o take the stage as a public speaker:

- Keep the stage lights working 50% of their full potential only.

- Imagine people with their vulnerabilities.

- Remind yourself that they are just 'people.'

s a leader:

- Be courageous.

- Be vulnerable.

Rumble with courage and vulnerability

our Skills of Courage

- Rumble/have meetings while staying vulnerable.

- Live in accord with your values.

- Give rise to trust.

- Learn to rise no matter the fall

2. Develop self-awareness and compassion

3. Spread courage by making tough decisions

Core Leadership Lessons

- Adopt a 'meeting minutes process' so that everyor understands what the meeting is about.
- Rumble with all team members to estimate timelines an deadlines. Using 'Post-it' notes is one example.
- Avoid stereotypes and binary thinking.
- Apologize for your mistakes.

To be a Daring Leader

- Avoid perfectionism and encourage healthy striving, sel compassion and empathy.
- Avoid dreading. Practice gratitude and celebrate wins an milestones.
- Avoid numbing. Set boundaries and find real comfort.
- Avoid binary thinking and manners. Practice integration an bring your wild heart, soft front and strong back together.

- Don't try to know it all. Be a learner.

- Avoid sarcasm and cynicism. Be clear and kind. Express what you mean and mean what you communicate. Nurture hope.

- Avoid nostalgia and the invisible army. Contribute and take risks as a leader.

- Avoid using 'power over' dynamics. Use 'power with', 'power to' and 'power within' equations instead.

- Avoid hustling. Comprehend your worth. Discuss every team member's contributions.

- Avoid trying to make people comply and control. Inspire commitment and shared purpose.

- Avoid exploiting fear. Acknowledge, name and normalize collective fear.

- Avoid promoting exhaustion and sleeplessness .Promote rest, play and recovery.

- Avoid discrimination, fitting-in and seeking approval. Endorse real belonging, inclusivity and diversity.

- Don't seek medals. Reward others.

- Don't avoid the hard thing. Do what needs to be done.

- Don't lead from hurt. Don't lead others to compensate for the gaps in your life. Lead from the heart.

Questions about the Book

What is the most significant message of the book?

Why is it important to rumble with vulnerability?

What are the four skill sets of courage?

What are the sixteen differences between armored and darin leadership?

What is the importance of grounded confidence?

What are the features of the 'Braving Inventory'?

Why should we avoid 'power over' dynamics?

How should we treat our values?

What are confabulations?

Check out other summaries

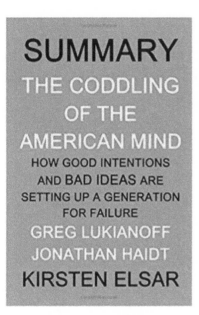

THANKS FOR READING!

CPSIA information can be obtained
at www.ICGtesting.com
Printed in the USA
LVHW091354240119
605122LV00001B/93/P

9 781790 547302